biopic

biopic | iggy pop

GAVIN EVANS

CANONGATE

First published in the UK in 2003 by
Canongate Books, 14 High Street, Edinburgh EH1 1TE
Published simultaneously in the United States of America and Canada
by Canongate Books, 841 Broadway, New York, NY 10003

10 9 8 7 6 5 4 3 2 1

ISBN 1 84195 445 4

Printed by Book Print, S.L., Barcelona
Thanks to Judy Blame for his understated genius

www.canongate.net

The portrait photograph is said to distil the sitter's essence. The photographer's role is to divine the subject's true character and present this truth to the audience in one immaculate shot. Talk of 'the decisive moment', or of capturing the sitter 'off-beat', only serve to strengthen the sense that there is only one all encompassing truth. In reality, portraiture does not work like this. There is no one truth. There is no one defining image, no one decisive moment. Today's sitters understand the power of the image and use this to make an impact on what is revealed. Who's framing who?

What portraiture fails to conceal, however, is the relationship between photographer and subject. It is their tale of reflex, reaction, intuition and psychology. As the story of the subject influences the photographer, the stories of those behind the camera influence the images created. The photographer is in every way a part of the image - as visible as the sitter. It is a documentation of their meeting, and it is their combined story.

I am the biographer of these moments. The story is Biopic.

2pm
Tuesday 15th October
1996
NYC

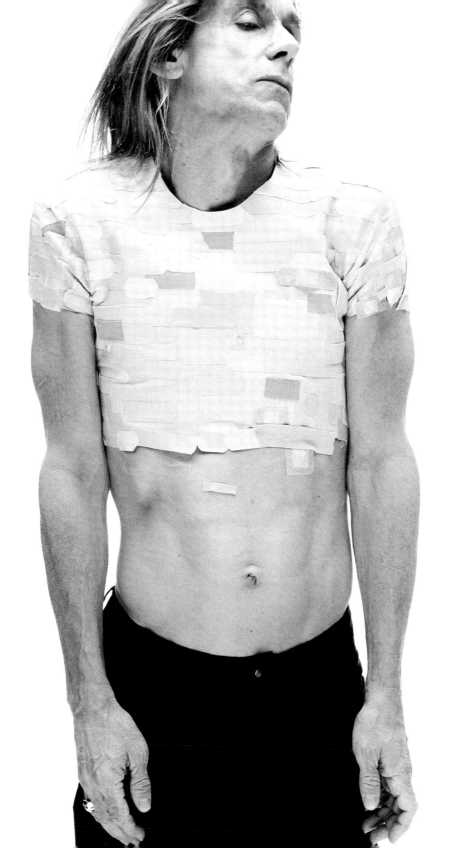

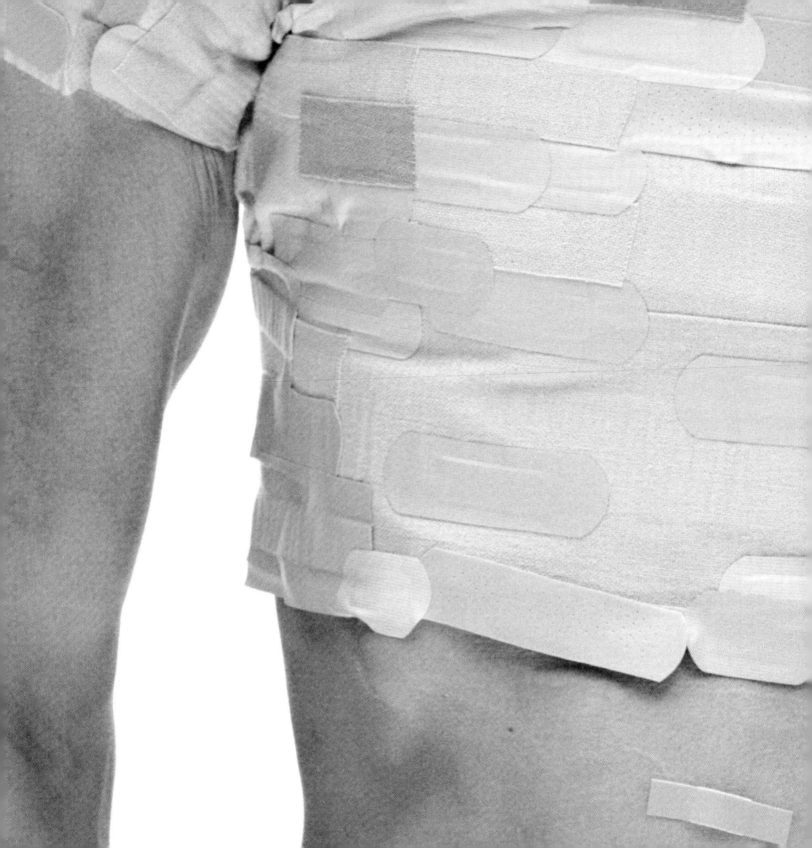

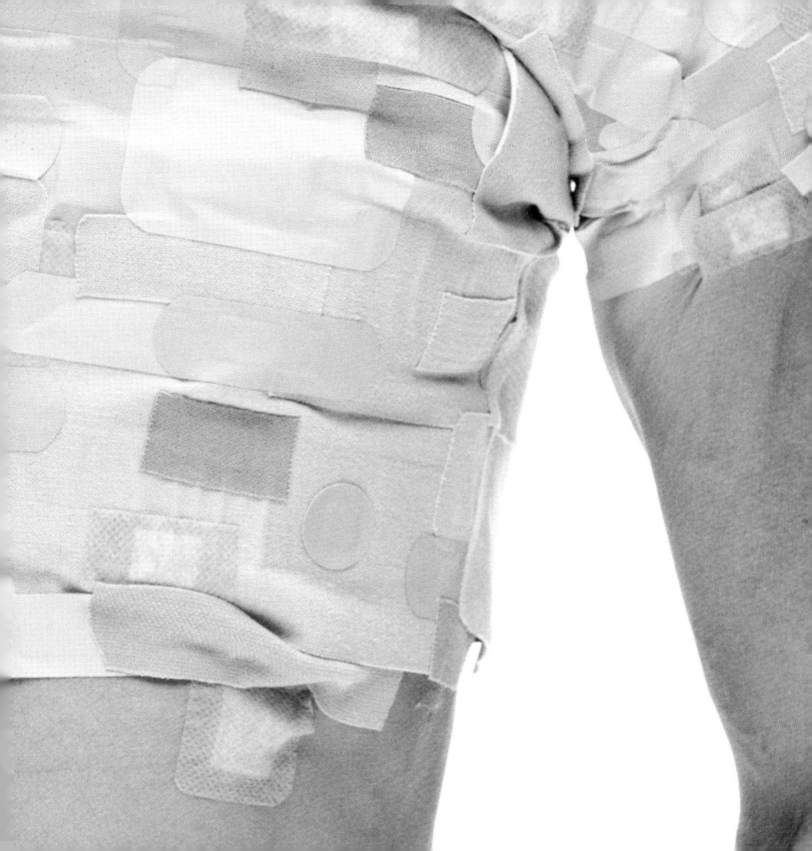

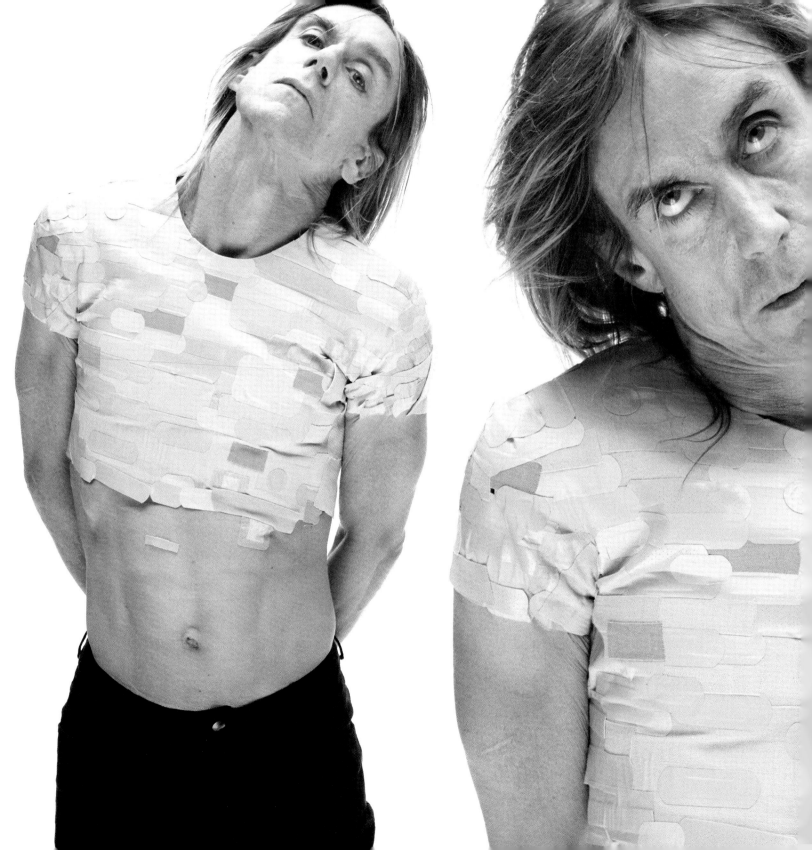

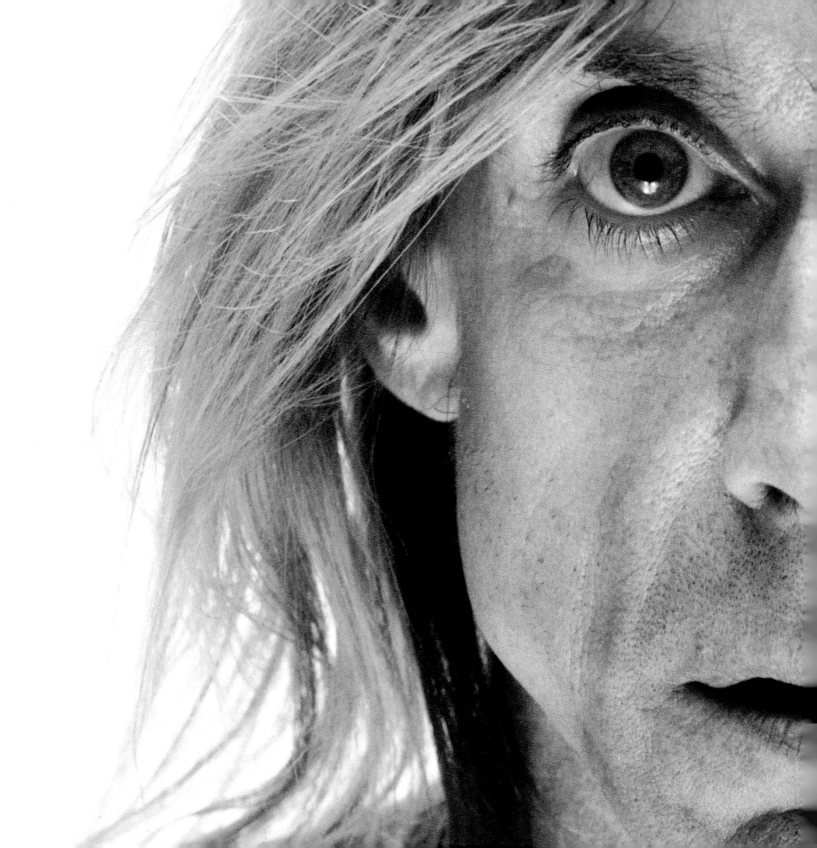

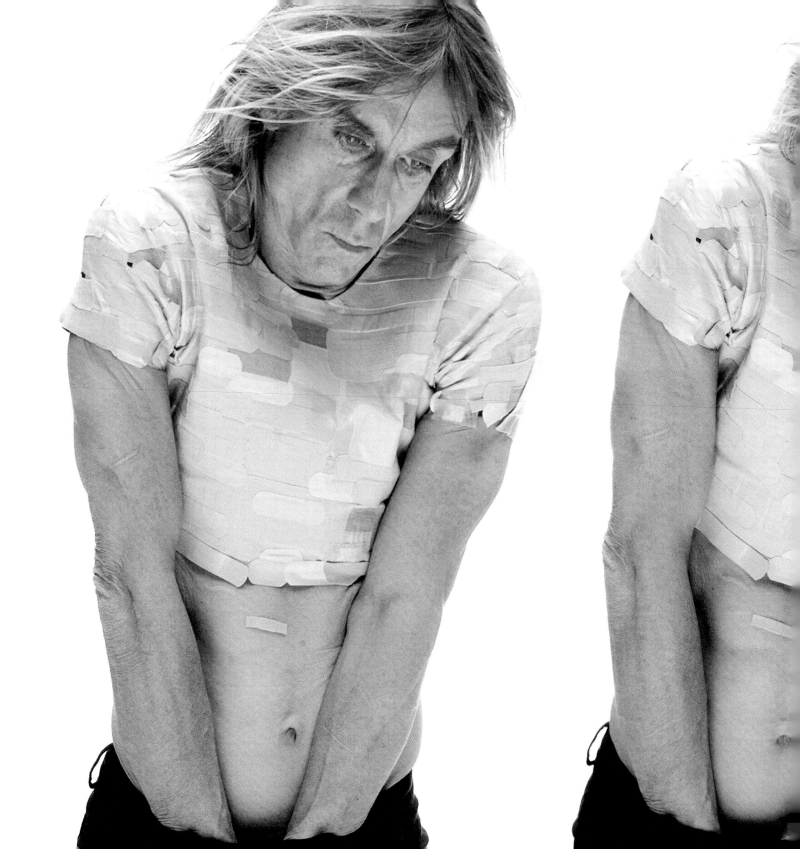

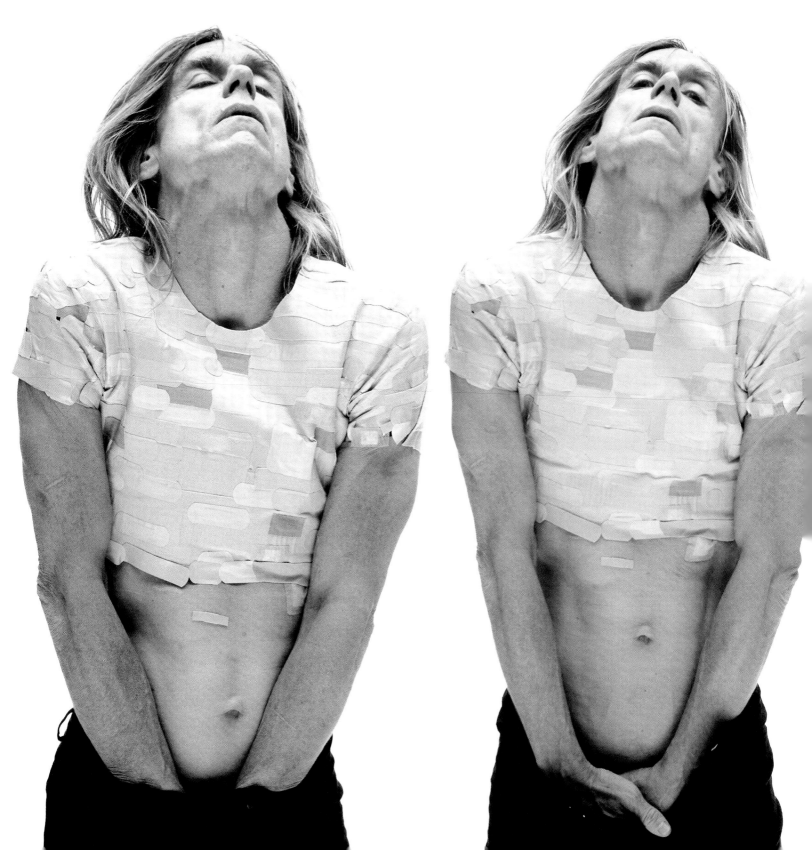

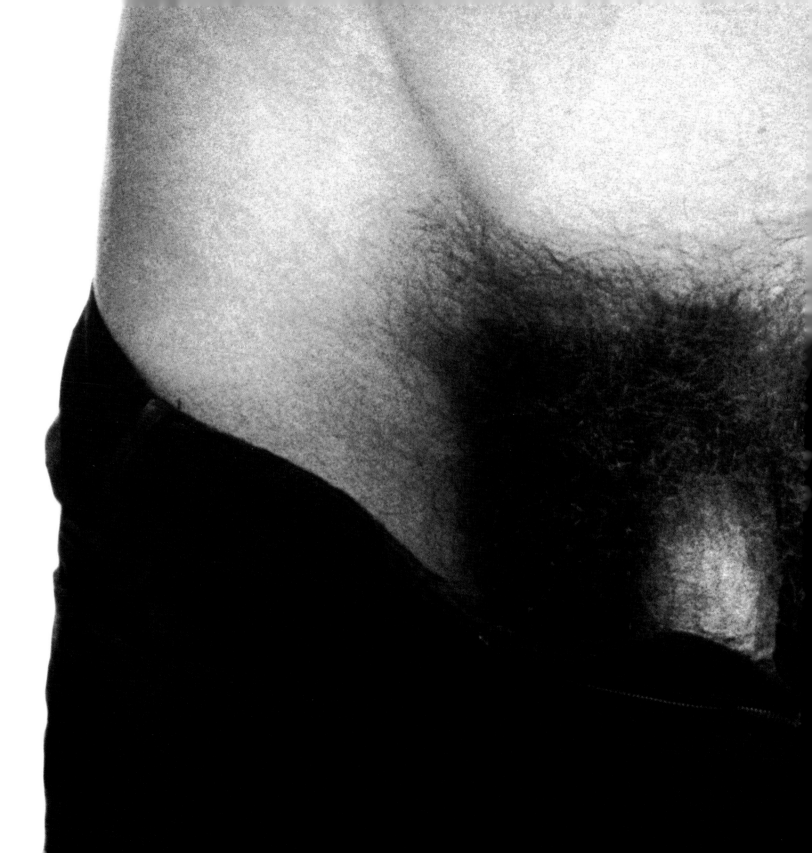

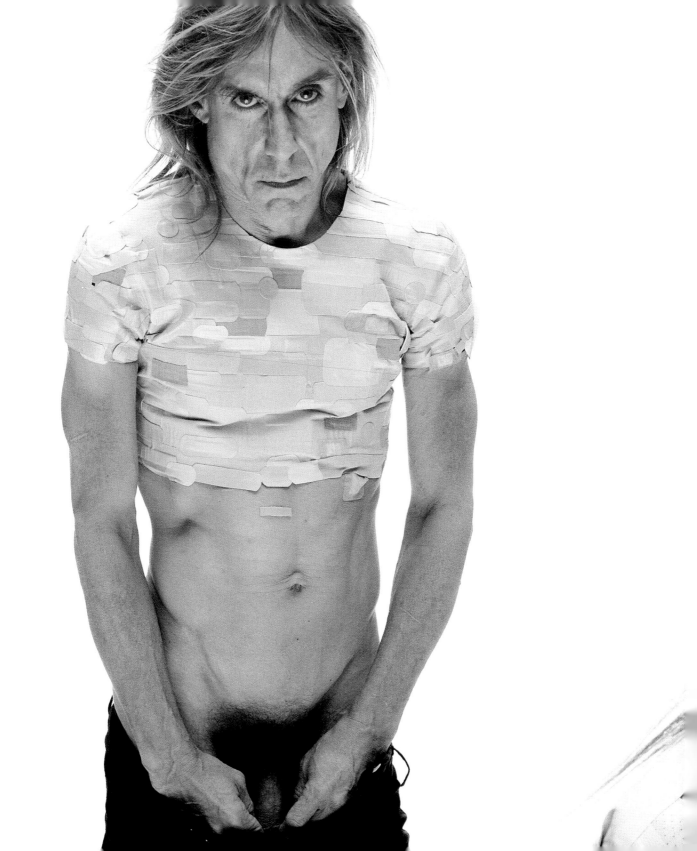

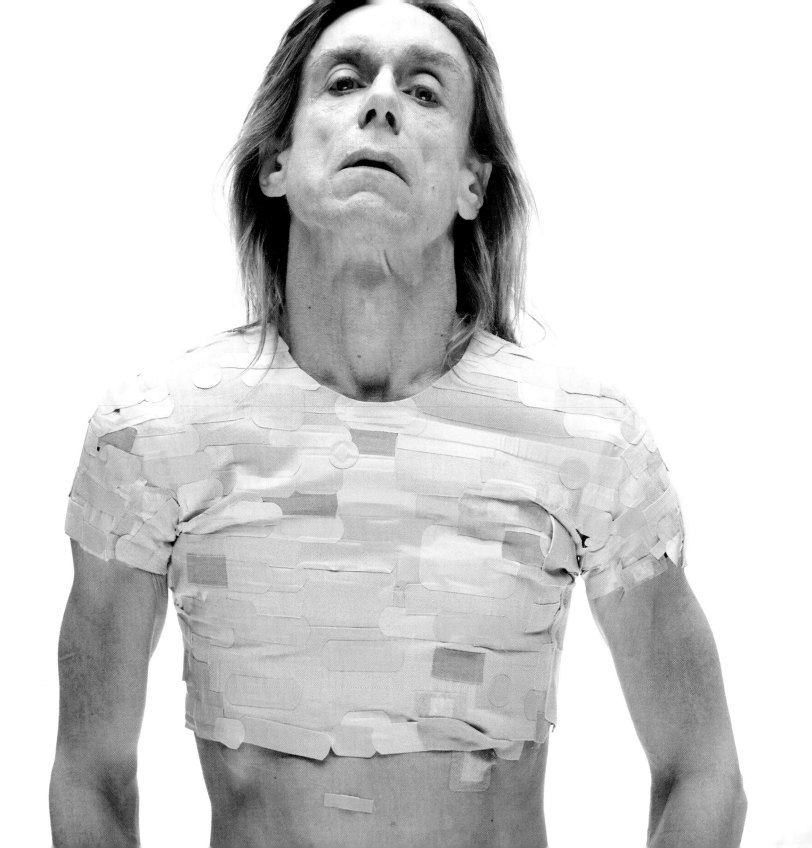

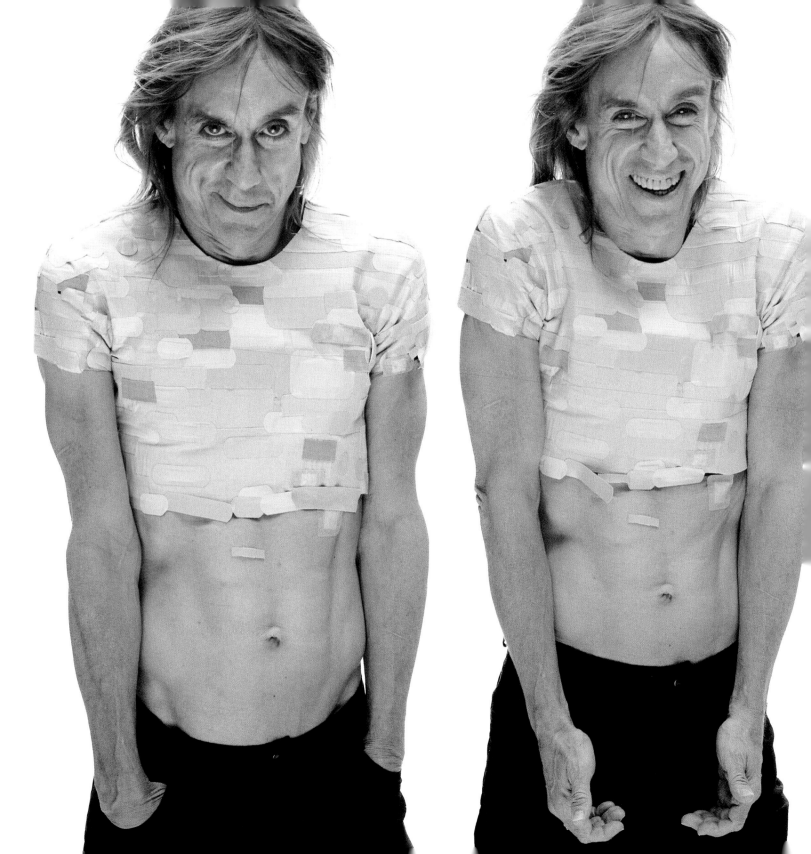

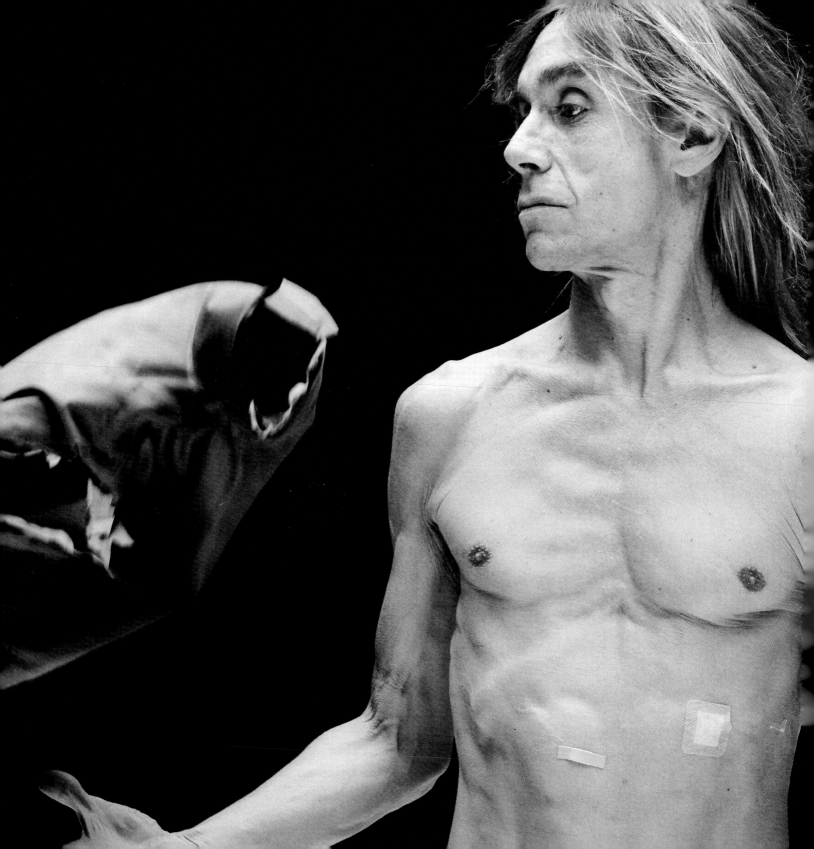

fuck rrrrrrr-
ker fuck
yuuuu uuuuuuu
bitchbitch   h,,
scarics .
Drin bring.
sex uuuuuuuuuuyo
sex uuuu
)))))) XXXX
sexsex   sex   sex   sexsexXXX
sexsex   sex.   iiiiiiiiii
sexsexex
sexsexex
you..uu uuuu
ck
fuckff f   sexsexse se

rı ı r r rr

uuu u u b i tch

b

HYSTERICS.   be

fuck.

rare bitch

x xx xxxbbbb

fuckerrrrrrr

our rare

sexsex

xxxxxx

bitch

bitch

ch b

ysterics.

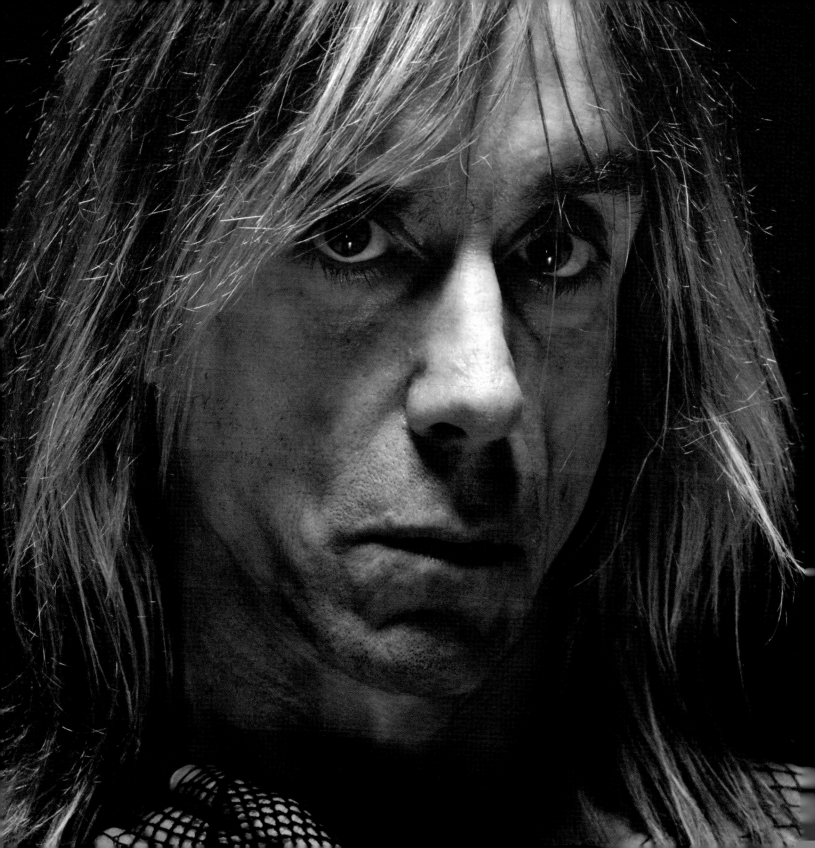

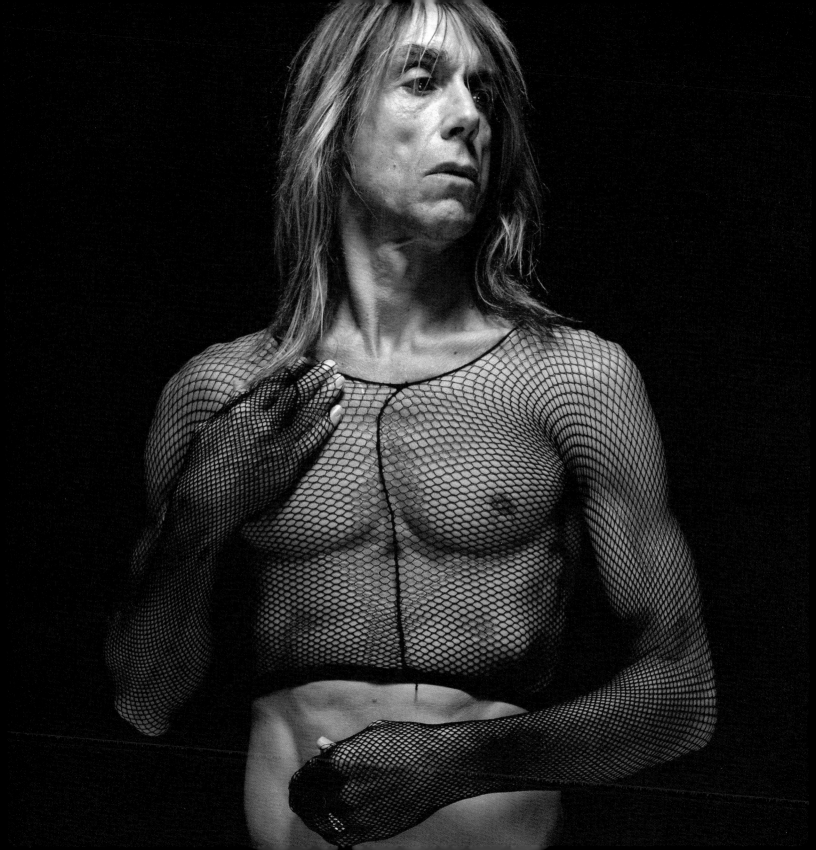

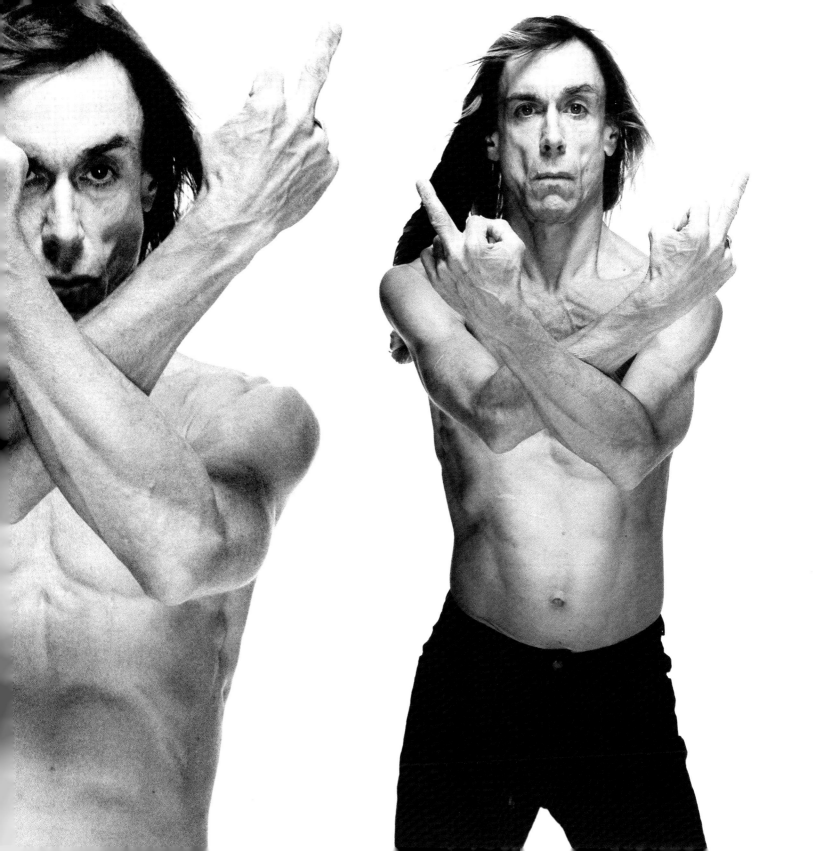

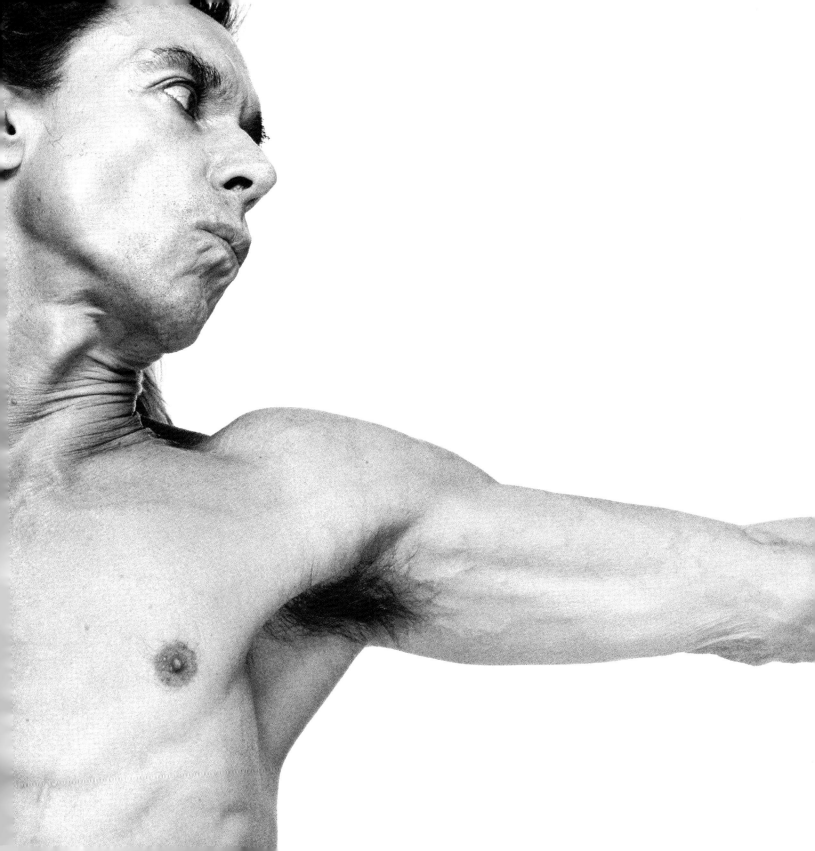

www.gavinevans.com